The Shopify Blueprint: 6 Steps to Building a Dropshipping Business

by

Alessandro

Table of Contents

Introduction	**5**
Before You Start	6
The Basics of Dropshipping	**9**
The Dropshipping Supply Chain	9
The Dropshopping Process	11
Advantages and Disadvantages of Dropshipping	12
Advantages of Dropshipping	13
Disadvantages of Dropshipping	15
Setting Up Your Dropshipping Business	**17**
Step 1: Lay the Foundation	17
Step 2: Set Up Your Store	17
Step 3: Look For and Contact Potential Suppliers	18
Step 4: Identify Products to Sell, Pricing, and Product Pages	18
Step 5: Finalize Your Set Up and Launch	19
Step 6: Advertising and Promotion	20
Step 1: Lay the Foundation	**21**
Identify your Niche	**21**
What Is A Niche Market?	21
Google Keyword Tool	23
Google Trends	24
Establish Your Brand	**25**
Step 2: Set Up Your Store	**27**
Understanding Shopify	**27**
Features of Shopify	**28**

Expectations of Shopify	29
Transaction Fraud and Security Issues	31
Dealing with Chargebacks	32
Shopify Apps	33
Orbelo	37
Integrating Orbelo with Shopify	37
Step 3: Finding and Contacting Potential Suppliers	39
Spotting Fake Dropshipping Suppliers	39
Identifying Legitimate Dropshipping Suppliers	40
Getting in Contact with Wholesale Suppliers	41
Before you Contact Suppliers...	45
How to Spot a Good Supplier	47
Paying Your Suppliers	49
Step 4: Identify Products to Sell, Pricing, and Product Pages	51
What Sort of Items Can You Drop Ship?	51
Choosing your Dropshipping Products	52
Step 5: Finalize Your Set Up and Launch	59
Use Social Media to Connect and Interact with your Target Market	59
Google Analytics	60
Test, Test, and Test the System Again	60
Customer Service Tips	61
Tips for Optimizing Shipping Costs	62
Step 6: Advertising and Promotion	64
Choose Profitable Source of Traffic	64
Build Website Authority and Credibility with SEO	65
Email Marketing	68
Social Media	68

| Facebook Ads | 69 |
| Conclusion | 70 |

Introduction

With most business having a presence on the Internet, e-commerce is getting bigger than ever with over two trillion dollars transacted online since 2016. This figure makes up more than 10% of total retail sales worldwide, and is expected to grow to 15% by 2020 according to a study done by eMarketer.

With e-commerce transactions can be conducted over the internet in milliseconds and there are no geographical restrictions. You can sell your product to anyone, anywhere in the world!

There are two ways that businesses can make money online. The first is purchasing inventory, which requires costs such as warehousing and order fulfillment. This method has large initial set up cost. The second method is using dropshipping. This is a business model where an e-commerce store owner simply lists the product on their site, while inventory and fulfillment is outsourced to another business. This removes the costs and hassle of managing inventory, as well as reduces the capital needed to start a business.

While the more common methods of dropshipping is using eBay and Amazon, the issue is that there is a large number of people using this method and the margins tend to be small. Additionally, the fees that eBay charges sellers will reduce profits. Instead of this, we will look at how to create a store with Shopify, automate it using an app called Oberlo, and then drop ship the item from Aliexpress. With a few clicks, the items ordered are paid for and shipped directly to the customer. It is common for such stores to have profit margins of 50% or more!

The dropshipping model features many benefits accompanied with variety of complexness and issues that we will explore in this book. With the knowledge in this book and careful preparation, you will be well equipped to handle most of the challenges you would encounter and you will be able to set up a successful, profitable dropshipping business.

Before You Start

If you really want to venture into the dropshipping business and profit on Shopify, take note of the road ahead.

Keep Expectations Realistic

Like any other businesses in the world today, setting up a dropshipping store requires a readiness to work with a view months if not years ahead. If you are anticipating a six figure monthly income or more with dropshipping, you are very likely going to end up disillusioned. Face your business with realistic prospects and projects about finances, sales, and profits that can be yielded.

If you are going into Shopify to be a drop shipper, you are going to need to put in a lot in form of the two not readily available currencies which are time and money.

Monetary Investment

While it is expected that you will need to spend money to put up and improve a dropshipping business on Shopify, it should be stressed that you need to be sensible about how the money is spent. Instead of putting in more money into a store just starting out, do most of the dirty work yourself to learn the platform, the market, and your customers. Without possessing enough knowledge of what you are dealing with, you get to be tossed around and you might get cheated by web programmers & developers, marketers and the likes. It is not mandatory that you do everything yourself, in fact most dropshippers outsource a fair bit of their busiess, but be sure you are the real and main driving force at the starting time of your project.

However, this doesn't mean you should not or will not spend at all. You will need some cash to kick off the business. Expenses that would need to be covered are those concerning web hosts and suppliers as well as feeds for Shopify and any other apps you decide to implement. As costs may vary and change over time, it is best to do your research before plunging in.

Time Investment

Investing time in your business, especially if you are new to dropshipping, is important.

- Keeps you updated and informed of the business. This enables you to scale your business as it grows.
- Creates a relationship between you, and the customers. This develops your knowledge of the market.
- By understanding the intricacies of your dropshipping business, you better understand which ventures are potentially going to be of a benefit to your business growth. You can better invest your time and money in this direction.
- Acquisition of new skills to better develop your entrepreneurship senses.

Dropshipping on Shopify might at the beginning might take lot of labor relative to small pay check, but you should bear some things in mind:

1. The dropshipping business on Shopify is more than just an income generating system but in a way, you are establishing a valuable possession that you can put up for sale later on in the future. Be certain to put into consideration the value of stake you are going to acquire alongside the income flow produced as end profit.

2. The moment you kick start your dropshipping business on Shopify, keeping it up will require a substantially reduced time compared to a 40 hour job every week. Many of your funds for investment will yield in the likes of competency and measurability offered when it comes to dropshipping on Shopify.

The Basics of Dropshipping

Dropshipping is a type of retail fulfillment, a method where a particular store does not keep the products it sells in stock. But instead, when the store is required to make sales of a product, it goes to purchase the item from a third party and from there has it shipped directly to the customer. Doing this, the seller never sees or gets his hands on the product.

With the easy access to the internet, it has become one of the choices for sellers to use dropshipping. The main difference between dropshipping and the standard retail models is that the seller does not hold any stock or inventory, reducing his costs. Instead, the seller goes to purchase the inventory as required from a third party supplier, be it a wholesaler or manufacturer so as to fulfill orders.

The Dropshipping Supply Chain

The "supply chain" is a puffed term used to describe the path followed by a product all the way from design through production then finally finding its way to the customer's hands. If we were to ask top supplier chain tycoons, they would establish that the supply of a product go all the way to the harnessing of the materials – such as the rubber and oil – put into use during the time of the manufacturing of the item.

That would be taking things too far and for the intent of this book we do not need to get intense. All you need to know is the three most relatable personnel making up this supply chain when it comes to dropshipping which are the: manufacturers, wholesalers, and retailers.

So let us run through the three players quickly:

Manufacturers – These set of people are in charge of the creation of the product and there are a few of those among them that make sales directly to the public. Mostly, they make sales in bulk to the other players in the chain which are the wholesalers and retailers.

Though buying products from the manufacturer is the cheapest form when it comes to purchase for resale, but many of them out there today have minimum purchase requirements put in place that you will need to meet. In addition, you will bear the responsibility of having to stock as well as reship the products when making sales to customers. This reason alone is enough to prove how easy it is to buy from the wholesaler and not directly from the manufacturer.

Wholesalers – The wholesalers make purchase of products in bulk from the manufacturers directly, have them slightly marked up and then have them resold to retailers – last players on the chain – to put up for sale for the public eyes. Wholesalers may set a minimum purchase requirement as well, but if they do you can be sure that it would be much lower compared to that which would be asked of you by the manufacturer.

The wholesalers go ahead to stock products from many – and sometimes hundreds – of manufacturers and very often run under a particular niche and perhaps, a particular industry. Most of them only make sales directly to the retailers and not to the public; they are known to be stringently wholesalers operators.

Retailer – A retailer is that person responsible for the sales of products to the general public at a somewhat increased price. You could be referred to as a retailer if your orders are completed through dropshipping suppliers in the business you run.

As you would notice, "dropshippers" do not appear as one of the players required and listed in the supply chain. The reason is not far-fetched and that is because any of the players – the manufacturer, wholesaler and even the retailer – can play the role of a drop shipper.

If a manufacturer decides to ship its manufactured products straight to the customer, it is called dropshipping, only that it is done your behalf. On the same note, a retail businessperson can render a dropshipping service, though at a non-competing price compared to that of the wholesaler which is because he is not being supplied directly from the product's manufacturer.

Being a dropshipper and getting the best pricing will require you make contacts with legitimate wholesalers or manufacturers.

The Dropshopping Process

The appeal of dropshipping is that it removes the cost of inventory management and allows businesses to focus on marketing the product. Once a sale is made, the order is passed to the supplier.
This is a fairly straightforward process and here are four basic steps to it:

1. **Generate interest through advertising and marketing, and receive customer orders.**

   In order to sell the product, you need to generate awareness by advertising and promoting the store and the products. You may do so on your website, on social media, or many other platforms. The goal is to drive traffic to your online store.

2. **Receive orders and payment.**

An order is started only when payment is made by customer, and you can proceed to process the order. The payment for the order should account for shipping cost, taking into account the weight and size of the item being sold.

3. **Forward the order to supplier.**

The item or items ordered needs to be purchased from the supplier, usually at a much lower price, and shipped to the customer. As you will receive payment for the order, you will need to pay the supplier for his order and shipping costs.

4. **Shipping the item.**

The supplier will process your order, and the item or items is prepared, packaged, and shipped directly to the customer.

Advantages and Disadvantages of Dropshipping

Online businesses has never been easier to start than it has gotten today with the uprising growth of shops such as Amazon, eBay, Shopify, and other retail platforms that exist online, making anyone with enough at hand start an online shop! Although the dropshipping model comes with a number of profits as well as benefits and disadvantages.

Many entrepreneurs want to get into this business as it has really low start-up costs.

Advantages of Dropshipping

Less Capital Required – Credibly the ability to establish an ecommerce shop without having to put in thousands in stock up front is now made possible. Conventionally, retailers have always had to get hands on large amount of capital purchasing stock.

When it comes to the dropshipping model, the product does not need to be purchased and kept in stock, the only time you need to make purchase is when you have been paid by a consumer and have already made the sale. It is now possible to start a productive dropshipping business with just a little cash without even having any major up-front stock assets.

Easy To Kick Start – Putting an ecommerce business into operation is much easier when you don't have to worry and deal with the products physically. In the dropshipping model, you can take your mind off a lot of worries such as:

- Renting or being in a charge of a warehouse.
- Packaging and shipping orders made.
- Keeping track of inventory for the reason of accounting.
- Taking charge of returns and incoming shipments.
- Making product orders repeatedly and managing stock level

Minimal Disbursement – Since you would not have to be dealing with and handling purchases of stock or keeping watch over a warehouse, your tax and expenditures are relatively low. It is no news that a lot of prospering dropshipping businesses are done from home offices with a laptop and without spending more than or up to $100 every month. As the business proceeds and grows, these costs might likely increase but will remain obviously minimal when compared to that of the conventional brick-and-mortar retail businesses.

Flexile Placements – The dropshipping business model can be activated and controlled from just anywhere at any time so long there long as there is an access to internet connection. All you need to be sure of is that you and your suppliers and customers alike can communicate easily without glitches, that being settled, your dropshipping business can be run and operated.

Wide Products Variety Available – You have the opportunity to offer variety of products up for display to all your promising customers, reason being that you do not have no pre-purchased items for sale. If your supplier – the wholesaler or manufacturer – adds an item to the inventory, you can place It up for sale on your e-market without extra cost.

Scaling Is Made Easy – Conventionally, in any business, if you are given two times the business you do on a regular basis you will actually need to work two times as much as you did on a single job. As an advantage in the dropshipping model businesses, the stress faced in processing of additional demands and orders is usually carried by the suppliers, leaving you with enough space to grow with minimal pains and less additive work stress. The prosperity of your business will always and surely come along with increasing tasks which are mostly customer related but it would be a business that makes appropriate use of scaling in dropshipping compared to the regular ecommerce businesses.

Without much doubt, all the benefits mentioned would make the dropshipping business a very attractive one to just beginning and already established businesspersons. Nevertheless, the dropshipping model is not all treasures at the end of the rainbow. There is a price to be paid for all the luxury and flexibleness involved.

Profit From The First Order Made – Most dropshipping suppliers are selling their products at wholesale prices. Together with low startup costs, this means that you will stand to gain from a single order. Your profit is the difference in the wholesale and the retail price, with margins of anywhere between 5% and 200% or more. Most dropshipping stores report average margins of between 30% to 70%.

Disadvantages of Dropshipping

Issues Regarding Stocking – It would be somewhat simple to monitor what items are available in surplus and those that are out of stock, if and only if you were responsible for stocking all your items. But when you source from various stores and warehouses this is not possible. Ways have been invented to help merchants better adjust your Shopify store's inventory with that of your suppliers', but these methods do not always work consistently and orderly due to the fact that not all suppliers support the required piece of technology.

Complexity In Transportation – If you follow the path of most drop shippers and end up working with a lot of suppliers, the products on your Shopify store will not be sourced directly but through a variety of suppliers.

As a result shipping costs gets complicated through this due to the order being shipped from different factories or warehouses in multiple packages. You will incur multiple shipping charges just to get the order delivered to the customer; it would be unwise to charge the customer for these numerous shippings because you would leave them with an impression that you are glaringly overcharging them for shipping!

Dropping Margins – The biggest drawback that can be faced in the dropshipping model is a low or dropping profit margin which happens when you operate in a niche that is established or competitive. As there are low barries to entry, competitors will appear and this puts a pressure on prices. Fortunately, it is possible to guard against competition.

Supplier Error –When suppliers make an error you will end up taking responsibility for the mistake. No matter how professional any dropshipping supplier might be, some instances come in place when there might be a mistake or fault in meeting demands of customers. You have no choice other than to accept responsibility and render an apology and sometimes a refund. This is why it is important to select your suppliers carefully to reduce letdowns such as missing items, wrong delivery addresses, or bad packaging resulting in damaged items. These will affect your credibility especially when customers share these stories on social media.

Setting Up Your Dropshipping Business

There are six steps to setting up your own dropshipping business

Step 1: Lay the Foundation

Identify Your Niche

Being passionate about starting your own business is awesome, but you need to start doing the hard work from day one. This is important because you do not want to be engaging in a business that does not have a market or one that has too many competitors. This means you have to do some research.

Establish Your Brand

You need to do this early on so that your brand becomes the compass for your business. This distinguishes your products and website from other competitors, and allows you to build a following.

Step 2: Set Up Your Store

At this stage you need to:

Choose a platform – There are various e-commerce platforms that you can use in your dropshipping business. There are some critical factors that you have to consider, for example, how the platform integrates with your software, functionality and design requirements, etc. You can either go with an open-source platform like Magento or WooCommerce, or hosted platforms like BigCommerce and Shopify.

Install themes - This involves picking the layout and look of your online store. Some themes come at a price while others are free.
Set up the store – This is where you now edit the colors, images, logo, fonts, menus, etc.

Step 3: Look For and Contact Potential Suppliers

Now you have to search for a drop shipper who can supply products for your business. It is possible that there may not be any suppliers for your niche product, but since you still have the backup list of niche ideas, you have options.

This step involves using Google search operators, which is an advanced way of conducting searches

Step 4: Identify Products to Sell, Pricing, and Product Pages

Once you are satisfied with the design of your store, you then need to determine the kind of products you will be selling. You will have to identify the specific products, their prices, and create product pages.

It is best to set up the visuals of your store so that you end up choosing products that are a good fit for your brand to reach out to your intended market.

Pricing the products in your store need to be very carefully considered. The cost of products in your store is crucial because each niche is very competitive, and you will need to account for shipping, advertising and other costs as well. As dropshipping has a low barrier to entry are plenty of other entrepreneurs doing the same thing you are doing and selling the same or similar products.

However, you should not undercut yourself because this will affect profitability and your income. Even then, great marketing skills, good quality products, top-notch customer service and other interpersonal skills that you apply can help you maintain a reasonable price and still attract customers.

Step 5: Finalize Your Set Up and Launch

You have already done everything necessary to set up your dropshipping business and the only thing left is to launch. Your online store is not perfect, and it may take a while for you to achieve your dream of becoming a millionaire, but at least you will be earning some passive income.

Here are some of the final touches that you need to add:

Social Media – Create a social media presence for your store on social media platforms. Social media accounts are very important for marketing purposes and for interacting with your customers.

Install Google Analytics – You need to monitor the number of site visitors, purchases, and signups. Measuring customer data is critical to online business success.

Test the system – Try purchasing to see what problems there might be and get a feel of user experience. Confirm the Add Cart button, checkout funnel, and email confirmation are all functioning as required.

Launch – Your online dropshipping store is now ready! Go live and generate traffic to your store.

Step 6: Advertising and Promotion

There are various ways to attract visitors and potential customers. The most common ones are:

Search engine optimization (SEO) – This is a way to improve the visibility of a website online by organically going up the search rank in search engines such as Google. These lead to long term branding and is a cost effective way to bring traffic to your web store.

Email Marketing – Once you have traffic on your website you can get visitors to sign up for your newsletter for an incentive, such as a coupon codes or freebies on their next order, in exchange for their email address. This is a slow but otherwise low cost way to reach out to warm leads. People on your email list are already interested in your brand, your product, or have identified themselves as part of your niche.

Social Media – Social media is one of the greatest marketing tools of our time. The average American checks his or her social media pages constantly throughout the day. That's ongoing potential exposure for your site. A page for your business should have been created in Step 5, and interacting with your audience through posts, videos, and pictures helps to build your brand.

Facebook ads – Advertisements on the world's most popular social media platform may be costly, but often show results. Facebook ads have a huge reach with a comparatively low cost to traditional media, and is a quick way to boost the visibility of your website.

Step 1: Lay the Foundation

Identify your Niche

Niche selection can be difficult at times, especially if you are fixated specific idea. Starting an online dropshipping store needs a flash of inspiration, and switching gears from your other business or job is necessary. While the process of niche selection is predominantly a creative task, can be simplified when you learn to use the creative side of your brain together with the analytical side. As much as the creative side of the brain is needed for generating ideas, the analytical brain helps to determe if a niche is profitable.

What Is A Niche Market?

Before you start anything, you should know who you're targeting and if there's a high demand market. A niche market is a specific subset of a larger market where a customer with a set problem or problems have been identified.

For example, people who are health conscious is a huge market and includes sub-niches like weight loss programs, diets, fitness, and many others. It is possible to "niche down" from people who are health conscious, to people who are interested in fitness. From there it is possible to niche down again to people who are interested in running, and then again to people who are interested in running marathons.

Each level you niche down becomes more specific, and your target market shrinks. However, as your market shrinks, the competition lessens and there is a greater chance for your business or product to address the needs of the niche market. The more specific you are the better.

Here are some of the steps:

1. **Brainstorm some niche ideas** – You need to focus on a particular niche, especially one you are passionate about. Catering for a smaller subset of the market, e.g., CrossFit fans, vegetarians, or yoga lovers will help you create a business that can meet customer needs easily.

2. **Run a Google Keyword Planner search** – This tool will help you know how many searches people are conducting about a particular niche. This is how you know which products are popular.

3. **Run an Amazon search** – This will also help you identify which products are in great demand.

4. **Conduct social media research** – Use Facebook, YouTube, Twitter, or Reddit to see how your potential customers are interacting with your niche market. Also, identify influencers who have large audiences/followers in your niche.

5. **Pick a niche** – Use the data you have collected to decide which niche market you want to create a business around. Keep the rest of the data as a backup in case your chosen niche does not work out.

Google Keyword Tool

Google makes this information available to the public with its keyword tool. If you type in a phrase or a word, it will tell you how many people have searched for it that month.

That's the simple version, but some people have written entire training modules on how to use the keyword tool. We're not going to go into that much detail here, but here are three tips you should keep in mind to use it effectively:

MATCH TYPE: This tool lets you find exact, phrase, or broad types when it shows you search volumes. Most people use the exact match option, and it's the best one to use. It gives you a very accurate idea of the search volume for that keyword.

LONG-TAIL VARIATIONS: If you choose just a one- or two-word search term, you will get an incredible amount of results. By changing your searches to "long-tail" ones, or searches that are longer and more specific, you will get more accurate results based on what your customers will be looking for.

Make sure to remember this when you're searching for profitable niches and markets. A search term with several different high-volume variations shows a strong market with lots of options and variety. A search term that has a much lower volume for its long-tail searches isn't as good. If you want to know more about estimating traffic, take a look at the links in the resource section about finding niches with long-tail potential and estimating long-tail traffic.

SEARCH LOCATION: Pay attention to the difference between global search volumes and local search volumes, which can be limited to a country or customized to a region. If you plan on selling in the United States, only look at the local search volumes, since most of your customers will be found there rather than in the global results.

Google Trends

Google's keyword search can show you raw figures, but Google Trends can give you much more detailed information, such as:

POPULAR AND RISING TERMS: Trends can also give you an idea of which searches have become more popular, which ones are growing the fastest, and which related ones are also popular. When you are planning your SEO and marketing efforts, focusing on the popular and rising terms is a good idea.

SEARCH VOLUME OVER TIME: Trends can tell you if the niche you're interested in is experiencing growth, which is a good sign for your business. It does this by showing you the increase or decrease in search volume over time.

SEASONALITY: If your product is a seasonal one that deals with decreases and increases depending on the time of year, it is important that you understand these changes. The keyword tool displays result from that month only, so the search's popularity can be misleading depending on the time of year.

GEOGRAPHICAL CONCENTRATION: Trends also allows you to organize search results based on where they originated geographically. If you were looking to sell canoes or related equipment, it would make sense for you to choose a supplier based on proximity to those customers, who represent the majority of your base.

Before you decide to carry a product, you need to learn everything possible about its search volume. Google Trend can help with this by giving you geographic concentration, search volumes, seasonality, and high-level search trends. Understanding all of this information will help you focus your marketing efforts and avoid expensive mistakes.

Establish Your Brand

Having a good brand is important to being recognizable and distinguishable from the competition. This is dependent on the perceived value of the brand in the eyes of the customer, which encompasses their experience with your company and its products. Here are some of the things you need to consider when establishing your brand:

1. **Choose a name for your brand** – This will help customers identify your business.

2. **Think of a tagline** – Your tagline should be a summary of the unique value proposition of your business. For example, "Just Do It" is the tagline for Nike. It tells you what the company offers – the ability to achieve any sports feat when you wear their shoes.

3. **Make a logo** – This is a visual representation of your brand. You can make one yourself using templates from online sources, or outsourcing this to a freelancer.

4. **Pick a color pallet** – You need to make sure that every aspect of your website and products are consistent, especially the colors. You want to create a specific atmosphere and vibe on your website, so pick the colors wisely. A good designer working freelance can help you with this.

5. **Set up your About Us page** – This is the page that most visitors go to when they want to know more about you. Tell people your brand story so that they can identify with your business. Your brand story is what persuades people to buy from you. It makes them think about what their lives would be like without you and how your products will transform their lives. Your brand story should go beyond the About Us page and into your social media accounts, adverts, and even customer support.

The above is just a brief coverage on how to set up and establish the brand for your company; as branding is a discipline on its own, I highly recommend you read a more comprehensive book on the topic if you would like to know more.

Step 2: Set Up Your Store

Understanding Shopify

Shopify is a complete e-commerce platform for businesses that are looking to sell their products online. While there are many options for building a webpage, and just as many online payment solutions to choose from, Shopify takes all the hassle out of mixing and matching and puts all the tools for getting your online business up and running in one place.

Additionally, Shopify is a payment gateway which means it handles the transaction verification process required to ensure that those who pay for your goods via debit or credit card have the funds to complete the purchase. It also means they are responsible for the security concerns related to these transactions which can be both complicated and expensive for merchants to pursue themselves.

When it comes to deciding how you want to use Shopify, the first thing you will need to determine is if you want to create your site and then link it Shopify or if you are more interested in getting started as quickly, easily and cheaply as possible by using the basic store template that Shopify provides. While the option to create your site will certainly cost more, it will give you complete control over the customer experience which is an important consideration if the niche you are considering working with is extremely competitive.

Features of Shopify

If you are wondering why you should use Shopify to host your e-commerce store, here are some of the features that make it a great place to open your store:

Effortless To Begin – With Shopify it is easy to jump ahead and start listing all the products and items available with your supplier for sale.

Open View to A Lot of People – When you have your store fully functioning on Shopify, your store is accessible to a lot of buyers who frequently visit the Shopify website. Thousands and Millions will get to shuffle through your store, and the somewhat sturdy market system will make sure you get the right kind of price for the products put up for sale.

Favorable Listing Fees – This is a great advantage because unlike sites such as eBay, you would not need to pay lot of outrageous fees and so called "success fees" which can amount up to 10% or even higher of the prices of sales made on your product.

In the Shopify dropshopping business where margins are somewhat slim, you can be rest assured that charges like this will not eat into your profits.

Sales Platform Customization – Shopify has a host of free and paid apps, templates and themes. However, your store designs doesn't need to follow a particular trend or template, giving you the chance to be more professional and creative with how your website can appear.

Content Management System – A Content Management System (CMS), makes adding or editing products as easy as drag-and-drop. A CMS also allows you to track inventory and shipping/order fulfillment through partner sites. Shopify is also compatible with several direct pay systems, so you don't have to worry about customer payments being dropped.

Long Term Customer Relationship Is Established – Customers can always be looped more frequently if accessories are accompanied with the products like it has been discussed in earlier chapters of this guide. And this depends on how well you brand yourself, design your store and so on.

Affiliate Management – With Shopify, you can run your affiliate marketing campaigns. An affiliate link allows you, the store owner to post a link to another site. If a customer from your store clicks a link to another store and makes a purchase, you will get a small percentage of the profits from that sale.

Dashboards –Most of us don't like to talk numbers, but Shopify takes care of that too. With a click of your mouse on your dashboard, you can see how your SEO and products are performing and what kind of traffic you are generating. If you are a fan of Google Analytics, you can also use that program easily with your web-store.

Expectations of Shopify

When you start off with a basic Shopify site, you can expect something akin to a basic WordPress site but without any of the related plugins. This niche can be filled on the Shopify application store which offers numerous varieties of applications for either no charge or a one-time or monthly usage fee. Many of the most common and useful applications are available free of charge, and it is simply up to you to determine which ones are going to be right for you.

Likewise, when first starting off it is important to have a realistic understanding of how much space you will need for the pictures of the products you are going to be selling and budget accordingly. For new businesses, it is unlikely you will need more than 1 gigabyte of allotted space before you start looking to expand your product line. Shopify offers up numerous options when it comes to website creation but it is also possible to use any of the major CMS platforms including WordPress, Joomla or Drupal to create a unique looking site, though you will need to code, or pay someone to code, the site in such a way that it plays nice with Shopify.

If you are not able to supply the coding knowledge yourself, it is important to budget at least $2,000 for this project, with many more elaborate jobs easily doubly or tripling this rate. If you are going down this route, it is important to have a very clear idea of what you want the result to be as any changes are going to cost you dearly.

If you choose only to be connected to the Shopify network but not take advantage of their all in one service you will need to individually source all of the elements of your site including the site itself as well as any hosting and credit card transaction fees. The costs and hassles of working with several different companies add up quickly, which makes the basic Shopify solution the most cost-effective and easiest choice for many new online business owners to make.

When it comes to payment solutions, you will have the option of using Shopify Payments which will be built into your store and is powered by Stripe technology. If you don't like the sound of the rates outlined above, then you are free to look into a third party transaction verification service which will be a more convoluted process that will ultimately save those who use it time and money in the long run. Additionally, it is important to note that Shopify payments are not available in all regions as well.

The biggest downside for many of these third-party programs is that users are required to have a merchant account to qualify which can be a difficult process for small businesses who are already processing a fair amount of transactions but may not have the best overall credit history. Acquiring a merchant account is a complicated process which requires a detailed history of previous successful transactions your online business has conducted as well as proof of a successful business plan. Merchant accounts are given out by debit and credit card companies, and they are anxious to ensure that the transactions they verify are going to go through on the merchant level as well as the consumer one as they are the ones on the hook if it all falls apart.

Transaction Fraud and Security Issues

Fraudulent activities can easily be spotted by scrutinizing orders made, and such illegitimate orders can be flagged and investigated before they get shipped. The patterns listed below do not always represent fraudulent activities but when two or more are noticed, it might be worth looking into:

1. **Multiple Orders to the Same Shipping Address** – When multiple orders with different billing addresses have a common shipping address this is a common sign of a fraudulent order.

2. **Difference In Names** – When billing and shipping addresses carry different names, it could be a red flag to note in fraudulent orders. Even in gift purchase.

3. **Weird Email Addresses** – Most email addresses owned by people have some part of their names if not even all of it integrated one way or the other into their email address. But if you come across weird email addresses such as efehqfeg@hotmail.com, there is a high probability that this email address was made up for fraudulent purposes or is a sign of fraud.

4. **Facilitated Shipping** – Fraudsters most time since they are making payment for charges off someone else's card, will seldom pick the quickest which is sometimes the most expensive of all delivery methods so as to reduce the amount of time you have to notice them before the product gets delivered.

If an order is spotted and suspected as fraudulent then put a call through to the number placed in the order form since almost all fraudsters do not put up their real phone number when making an order. If the call goes through, be sure to have close to a 30 seconds discussion with the receiver and have everything verified. In some cases you can get a feedback message stating that the number does not exist, or a receiver who has no idea about the product ordered. If that be the case, you can cancel such orders and make a refund in order to avoid chargebacks or problems of any kind.

Dealing with Chargebacks

When a receiving customer puts a call through to his or her bank to enquire about a charge made by you, you will get to receive what is known as a chargeback. The processor in charge of your payment will deduct the amount of the charge in question from your account for a period of time, for you to provide proof that the goods and services in question was delivered by you to the customer. If you fail to provide these proofs, you will get lose the amount of disputed charge including a charge for a chargeback processing fee. If you end up accumulating too many chargebacks in your Shopify drop shipping business relative to the amount of orders you have processed, you could end up losing your business account.

Chargebacks are mostly caused by fraudulent activities but you would be given a good and fair chance of recovering your funds so far as no untrue statements were made in the course of the made transaction.

However, if the chargeback is associated with an order carrying a different billing and shipping address, there is a low probability of you winning the dispute. You can only be compensated by your processor for the fraudulent orders shipped to the billing address on the card. Most times, it is advisable not to respond to those kind of chargebacks because it can be a total waste of time.

Shopify Apps

Shopify has several apps to enhance your business capabilities. Apps can make shopping easier for your customers and make the business side easier and more efficient for you to manage. Apps can be great for marketing. Using the right apps can make your site more easily findable in search engines. You can use apps for email marketing which will help get customers to your site.

Ask yourself a few important questions before delving into the app store. First, is there anything not already built into Shopify I need to be successful? How do I drive more traffic to my site? How can I make my store operate more easily? If I buy apps, how much will I budget for them? These questions provide valuable information for decision making.

There are free apps that may do the trick just fine for your store. If you decide a free app isn't sufficient for your growth after some time, you can always upgrade to a paid app.

A third party produces these paid apps. Some will offer a free trial which you can use to determine if that app fits your needs. Some offer to price based on functionality. The more you need from the app, the more you pay for it. There are also different pricing models such as per use or a flat monthly rate. There also are one-time pay apps. Just remember, if you choose monthly billing apps, they may charge you automatically. If your store closes, it is possible you will still be billed for those apps. Make sure before purchasing an app that you understand the terms & conditions.

Here are a few of the awesome apps found on Shopify to help you grow your business and make more money. Some are free, and some have rates that may apply.

The SEO Image Optimizer helps your images show up in a google search under the images tab. There are other SEO apps as well. Search Engine Optimization is important to your ranking in search engines, as we will discuss in a later chapter.

Coupon apps can help create email lists as well as bring customers back to your store.

There are social feed apps also. These apps are set up to post directly to your favorite social media pages. You can also have your social media feed directly loaded to your store. Either option will bring more visibility to your site and more potential customers.

While every store owner has their preferences in apps, there are some that seem to be rated very highly by many store owners. Here are some of the best apps available on Shopify:

Loyalty Points by Bold offers customers the opportunity to earn points redeemable for purchases at your store. This is a great way to keep your customers coming back.

As the store owner, you can determine the number of points a customer earns. For instance, you can have different loyalty levels, each earning more points for given purposes. You can also place the number of points needed to purchase an item right along with the dollar price to entice customers to buy more often to earn points.

Better Coupon Box is a great way to keep your bounce rate low. The bounce rate is based on visitors to your site who do not buy and never come back. Adding a discount just for following you on social media helps drive sales.

The creators of Better Coupon Box have made it very user-friendly. It works wonderfully on various media devices. You can grow your followers and likes on Twitter, Instagram, Twitter and any other social media.

Since we now live in a mobile world, isn't it only natural your customers want a mobile shopping experience? **SellMob** allows your customers just that. With both iOS and Android capabilities, SellMob will get your conversion rates pumping with a wonderfully fluid mobile app.

MailBot will convert visitors into repeat customers. Let an automated email bring customers back with exciting offers and discount coupons for loyal customers. The folks at MailBot will help you send out targeted emails to your customers.

Have you ever ordered an item online and had no way of knowing when it was to be delivered? With **Aftership**, your customers will never have to wonder. Aftership will allow shipment is tracking all in one place. You and your customers can rest assured in knowing where their packages are while in transit.

You can further increase repeat sales with Aftership by sending a follow-up email to your customers. You can use this to get a review of their shopping experience and to offer discounts for their next visit. Aftership has courier networks across the globe and a global support network.

Quick Quote allows a customer to load up their cart and then ask you directly for a quote. You may wonder how this is such a great idea. What is wrong with standard pricing you may ask. Nothing is wrong with standard pricing. There is also nothing wrong with turning a potential bounce into a paying customer.

If a customer asks you for a quote, this is a great opportunity to offer discounts for this purchase or a future purchase if it will get the customer to buy.

You can use Facebook Chat by **Beekeeting** to convert more customers. Using this app opens a whole new chapter in social networking. You can have a direct, live interaction with your customers/fans from anywhere using a mobile device. Using Facebook Chat by Beeketing, you can also review customer profiles and get to know them better. This will enable you to target your marketing more efficiently.

Conversions is somewhat of an all-in-one app. With it, you can send emails and newsletters. You can make recommendations based on customer buying history. You set up a search on your site so customers can go directly to the items they want to buy.

If SEO is not your strong point or if you just don't want to have to do it and would rather let someone else take care of that for you, **Alt Text** is a must have. This app will make the best use of alternate keywords to drive your search engine ranking higher. Let the experts do the work for you.

Bulk Discounts is a Shopify app which helps you create multiple discount codes in a short amount of time with limited effort. It doesn't just help build discount codes; it also allows you to track the use of discounts, delete discounts, track discount conversion rates, and more.

Orbelo

The Oberlo app enables you to import products from AliExpress to your store to drop ship; Items sold in your store can be shipped directly to your customers in just a few clicks. *Note that Orbelo does not work with any other directory or portal except AliExpress*. Oberlo also includes pricing auto-updates, shipment tracking, and many other features.

Oberlo will track the progress of the order and notify you if the order is taking too long. If the order is not shipped within the processing window listed by the seller, you have to option to have the order refunded. Once an order is shipped, you should get a "tracking code," but it can take a few days.

Integrating Orbelo with Shopify

The moment that you have figured out the sort of design you want on your Shopify store for dropshipping, it will be required of you to begin to add items and products, so as to start generating profits and revenue. If you want to add drop-shippable items, you will need to get the Oberlo app installed. Oberlo is one of the platforms – in fact, it is the leading platform – for ecommerce merchants who would like to have dropshipped products imported to their dropshipping store on Shopify. Shopify is seamlessly incorporated with Oberlo in a way, making it possible to import and offer products from the starting day of your business.

Oberlo can be easily connected to your already existing Shopify account to an Oberlo account, and it understands that the stages of managing inventory to meeting order fulfilment is a lot of work to do; therefore Oberlo creates various ways in which you can fulfil orders from your Shopify store on your Oberlo integrated app.

1. **Fulfilling Orders Using the Tracking Code** – On Oberlo, after getting your Shopify store integrated, you can readily click on the **"Get Tracking Code"** next to any placed order. This sends the tracking code of the product from the suppliers website ordered from to Oberlo immediately.

2. **Fulfilling order through other various buttons** – On the orders page of your Oberlo website, you can fulfill a single order by clicking the **"Send Details"** tab but if you want to fulfill orders in bulk then make use of the **"Sync This Page"** or **"Sync All Orders"** tab. That being done, all your orders' information will be transferred to the Oberlo application for accessibility.

3. **Getting Orders Fulfilled Manually** – After your order has been shipped and the tracking information has been given to you, go over to the Oberlo website then to the **"Orders Page"** and click the **"Mark as Shipped"** button next to the order in question. You will get a pop-up window where you would paste the copied tracking code information.

Step 3: Finding and Contacting Potential Suppliers

Before going out on a wild search for suppliers it would be important to identify how to spot the differences between valid wholesale suppliers and inferior retail outlets displaying themselves as wholesale suppliers. This is necessary because the true wholesalers get their stock directly from the manufacturer and will usually not have a problem offering you glaringly better pricing.

Spotting Fake Dropshipping Suppliers

It is not surprising or difficult to come across an outraging lot of fake wholesalers, though it might depend on the places you find yourself searching. It is so painful that the legal and valid wholesalers are conventionally bad at marketing and publicity therefore making them even harder to find. As a result, we experience these mere middlemen and counterfeit wholesalers appearing more oftenin your search results. This is a signal that you have to be cautious to a fault.

There are tactics that would help to an extent in identifying this sort of non-genuine set of wholesalers:

Sales Are Made to The Public – To begin business transactions with a valid wholesaler and get access to wholesale pricing one must need to apply to own a wholesale account, pass through screening in order to prove that you are a valid businessperson and get verified before you can even go ahead in making your first order. If you come across any so called "wholesale" supplier offering products to the public at large at "wholesale prices" then do not fall victim because it is just a retailer giving items for sale at an inflated price.

They Charge Service Fees – The legit wholesalers do not place silly charges on their customers under tags such as a "monthly fee" for the permit of doing business and making orders from them. If you are requested by any "wholesaler" to make payment for a service fee or monthly membership renewal then, there is a probability that it is not legit.

It is of great importance at this stage, especially if you want to become a drop shipper on Shopify to discern between suppliers and supplier directories (this term will be discussed as we move on).

Wholesale suppliers possess some sort of directory that is organized by either market or types of product and that are passed through screening in an effort to ensure the legitimacy of suppliers. This is known as supplier directories. For most of this type of directories, an ongoing fee or a one-time fee will be charged, depending on the directories pricing plan, so don't go thinking this is a red flag indicating the directory itself is invalid or illegitimate.

Identifying Legitimate Dropshipping Suppliers

Just as there are ways in which you can point out the illegitimate wholesalers among the lot, let us see if this guide can help you identify the valid and legitimate ones.

Per-Order Fees Request – A lot of drop shippers charge a shipping fee per-order that can go ranging from $2 all the way to $5 or more, but that depends on the size of the package to be shipped and complexness relating to the item. This standard has been established in the industry, resulting from the high cost of packing and shipping most orders individually which turns out to be higher that a bulk order shipment.

Established Order Size – Most if not almost all wholesalers have an established minimum order size, which you have to request for or purchase at your starting order. This is done in an effort to sieve out businesspersons that come to window shop, wasting their time with rhetoric questions and minute orders which in the end will not translate into a significant or productive business.

Getting in Contact with Wholesale Suppliers

Yes! You are now an expert at detecting a scam from a real deal, good for you, now it is time to go fish for suppliers for your Shopify store. There are numbers of tactics that can be put in place to achieve this, some being more productive or responsive than the others. The methods are listed from bottom to the top in the order of their responsiveness and effectualness which means the best method – from our point of view – is listed last:

Look-Up Directories

Of the questions asked by growing ecommerce business persons – or should we say entrepreneurs – the most common of them all is the one asking if they should go ahead to pay for a supplier directory…Though a suppliers' directory can turn out effective or helpful, they are not counted or tagged as necessary. If you have your mind made up on the niche to embark on or product you want to sell then it would be more advisable to find the biggest suppliers in your market niche with a bit of scavenging and putting the succeeding techniques into use. In addition, it would be good to note that once you embark on your business you will probably not find yourself visiting the directory anymore only if you need to find new suppliers for a different product or niche entirely.

But on a sincere note, supplier directories are one of the easiest ways to search for or browse a large number of suppliers which can be very useful and of help when you seem to be running out of time and would not mind spending the money to save you from the stress.

A great number of various supplier directories are out there but a detailed review of all of them would be going beyond the intent of this e-book. Nonetheless, we have got some of them [the most popular supplier directories on the web] highlighted below. Do well to note that none of the directories listed below are put up for recommendation or endorsement, the list is only given as a help saving you time you will go spending on numerous options.

- ➤ **AliExpress:** This directory has suppliers made up from small businesses, mostly from China, offering products internationally. AliExpress directly connects businesses with buyers, and is targeted to overseas buyers; as such customers in China are not allowed to buy from the website.

- ➤ **Worldwide Brands:** This directory is somewhat trusted costing a lifetime membership fee of $299, it has been used personally by Shopify themselves and they testified on their website saying:

> *"…We've used the directory in the past to find legitimate wholesalers… and found it very useful. Though the directory is missing some suppliers we've worked with, it does include a large collection of legitimate wholesalers…"*

The above testimony speaks a volume for the brand already.

- **SaleHoo:** The SaleHoo supplier directory lists 8000 – if not more than – dropshipping suppliers for just $67 on an annual basis. Their site has plenty of tools that you can use to customize your e-commerce site..

- **Wholesale Central:** Unlike the preceding directories, this supplier directory gives its service free of charge and this is because the suppliers listed are charged a fee in addition to ads that gets displayed on their website.

Order-from-the-Competition

Most times it can be difficult to locate suppliers, at this stage you might need to turn to antique order-from-the-competition method.

How does it Work? Get yourself a competitor that you suspect is also into dropshipping and place an order of minimum value. When the package is delivered, look up the return address on Google to identify who the original shipper was and luckily he might be a supplier that can be contacted.

This is a popular method in the market today and to an extent has been effective so far. Fortunately for you, you laid hands on a supplier using other techniques then you must have been lucky, maybe the market was not competitive and other factors. Notwithstanding, bear this technique in mind but never commit the mistake of going on to rely on it completely.

Search Using Google

The big brother and all-knowing Google can also be used to find high-quality suppliers but mind you, there are a few things to bear in mind. As discussed earlier in preceding chapters, Wholesalers are poor at publicity and marketing so to find them – the legitimate ones – you are going to need to search extensively because you would not expect them to appear among the top search results or neither should you expect to see them on the first ten pages. You would have to hunt through hundreds of Google search result pages if you are looking for "legit" in your Shopify dropshipping business.

Be careful to also not judge by the website design no matter how seemingly old they might be. The legit wholesalers are known to have poor designed websites mostly featuring styles from the 90s. Therefore, where an eye-catching website depicts a real supplier in few cases, many legit wholesalers out there have a scary poor design but do not let that distract you.

Contact the Manufacturer
This is the surest way and also the most preferable way to get in touch with wholesale suppliers that would be valid and not counterfeit. Once you know the niche you are ready to invest in or the market product you want to sell, call the manufacturer and get a list of all the wholesale distributors available then further get in touch with the wholesalers questioning them of dropshipping services and make enquiries about setting up an account. With just a few calls made to leading manufacturers under your preferred niche, you will get safe and legit access to a sea of leading wholesalers in that market.

Before you Contact Suppliers...

If you followed the techniques given above, you should have gotten just enough suppliers' contact at hand now and you are all ready to take a step further to begin your own dropshippping business on Shopify. But just before you take that step of calling and reaching out to supplying companines, you will want to confirm that you are all set.

Get Yourself Legalized – As stated earlier in this guide, most valid wholesalers will require convincing proof to show that you are a legal businessperson before giving you room to register for an account. Many wholesalers out there today smartly display only their pricing to verified customers which means you need to be legally integrated if you really do want to see the kind of pricing available to pick from.

What all these means in essence is that before going ahead placing through to suppliers, you must be incorporated legally.

Be Careful How You Present Yourself – A lot of people with their "great business plans" are constantly available throwing question jabs at wholesalers, eating up a lot of time end up ordering nothing. This is experienced by wholesalers constantly so get it to your head that if you want to embark on a dropshipping business on Shopify then don't expect many or any of many of the suppliers go an inch out of their way to get you on your feet.

You might get lucky and come across suppliers who would be willing to set you up and give you a dropshipping account. If you fortunately get this kind of luck, do not go wild with joy asking for a discount in pricing or take hours window shopping and holding down their representatives on the phone for ages and end up making a single insignificant sale. It paints you with a bad repute and ends up breaking every bonding relationship you might be having or developing with the supplier.

To convince a supplier to reduce pricing for dropshipping or to make other special demands or requests, you would have had to build an outstanding credibility. Be clear and succinct when defining business plans instead of off-the-wall rhetoric. Don't forget to discuss your past professional business successes which you might have had in the past that you think might interest the supplier and make them believe you have what it takes to succeed in your new venture maybe through sales, marketing or both.

Guarantee them with enough sturdy reasons of how their accommodation to your special inconvenient requests will pay off in the long run when it blooms and you start visiting them with a large volume of business deals. Make them believe in you.

Get on the Phone – Many people have no problem sending emails to their supplier, but hesitate to answer the phone a call comes from their supplier, similarly they feel the same unease when they have to call the supplier too. Often, you will need to pick up the phone for some piece of information or sort out issues with orders.

There is nothing bad about your supplier calling you. They send out calls to dropshipping gurus and newbie drop shippers as well. A tip to make things easier is to get all your questions written down beforehand, so when you are on the call you don't need to think too far, just a look at your pre-written questions and you are good to go. It gives you and the sales representative an easy and amazing time together.

How to Spot a Good Supplier

As it is with most of the things in the real life, not all suppliers are created equally. In the dropshipping world where the supplier is established to play the most crucial role in the area of order fulfilment, it is more than most valuable to be sure that you are working with first rate bodies.

Outstanding suppliers are known to possess some, if not all of the following features:

Knowledgeable Staff
First rate supplying bodies have staff and sales representatives with more than enough expertise about the industry and the lines of product handled. Though, calling a sales representative to ask questions relating to a niche or market product you know virtually nothing about or not over familiar with is totally invaluable.

Responsible Representatives as Support
Top-notch drop shippers should endeavor to delegate to you a particular sales representative that would be answerable to any questions or issues that you might have as well as see to the fact that you are being taken care of. When there is no delegated representative, it would be observed that problems take longer before they get looked into, most times you might have to nag them into working on an issue. This is why getting a contact assigned to you is extremely valuable.

Well Integrated Technology

Though we mentioned the case of good and legit suppliers with the '90s styled websites earlier, it is better to still/also note that any supplier that understands the benefits and puts a lot into acquiring the best grade of technology is worth working with. Access to a timely updated inventory, a well detailed online catalog, well defined data feeds and an order history that can be searched online really provide a sort of comfort for businesspersons on the web and can help you operate more efficiently.

Accept Orders through Email
As minor as it can seem, but it would be more time saving and productive to be able to call in every order or place it manually on the website.

Located At the Center
If you run your Shopify store in a large country, it would be of more benefit to identify a drop shipper that is located at the center of the country because most items can reach up to 90% - if not more than – of the country in a space of 2 or 3 working days. If a supplier stays out on the coasts, orders can take up to a week or more than to be shipped within the country. Suppliers that reside at the center of the country gives room for consistence in quick delivery times, readily helping you to save money when it comes to shipping fee charges.

Orderly and Proficient
Most item suppliers have legally qualified staff and efficient methods that turn out to produce a competent and wholly hitch-free fulfillment. Many others will make a mess of every order and keep you frustrated to the extent of pulling your tooth out of your mouth. And one problem is that it is almost or nearly impossible to establish the efficiency of a supplier only if you get to make use of their services.

This doesn't guarantee that you would get the clear picture of what a supplier really is at the first shipping but at least it gives a reasonable sense of the service a supplier offers. Giving you the chance to observe how the process of order fulfillment are handled, how fast items and packages gets shipped out, how quickly information and invoice are tracked and followed up, and lastly the quality of the item package when it arrives at customer's destination.

Paying Your Suppliers

Suppliers at large majorly accept payment in any of the two ways:

Credit Card
The credit card payment option is mostly required of newbies in the dropshipping business. After attaining a level of prosperity and success in the business, the credit card option still remains the best. Apart from this being a convenient option owing to the fact that you do not need to repeatedly or regularly have checks written, it also gives you the chance of racking up numerous rewards flier miles. The fact that you are making purchase of a product for a customer who has paid beforehand on your Shopifystore, you can go racking up significant amount of purchases using your credit card and not have to attract any precise non budgeted expense.

Invoice Net Terms
The other major and common mode of making payment to item suppliers is with the net terms on the invoice. This implies that you have been given a particular time frame or number of days within which you should pay your supplier for the purchased good which has been shipped out. Payments for the purchased goods can be made to the supplier either by check or bank draw.

On a normal note, your supplier will request that you provide credit references before opening the door of opportunity for you to make payments on the terms of net payment because it in a way looks like you are being given a loan. This is a conventional practice that have already been established, so there is no reason to panic when you are asked to provide certain documentations when on the terms of net payment.

Step 4: Identify Products to Sell, Pricing, and Product Pages

What Sort of Items Can You Drop Ship?

Many of you have heard about drop shipping. You might want to know what exactly can you drop ship? When we looked at this, we found that if you wanted to, you could drop ship almost anything. Here are a few things that we have found that people will work with.

One of the first things that we have found was that people were marketing furniture. Anything you could think about from dining room tables too much more were being drop shipped. There are other things than just that. Things that you have wanted for a while might be out there waiting for you to find them.

If you love your brand names, then you could find some great deals on things being marketed. Many others have a whole bunch of items. What are a few of these things?

One of the things that have been shipped is designer clothes. Not only can you get the brand names that you love such as Prada and Diesel among many others. You can also see some great savings. People have noticed that when they buy things as they are dropped shipped; you can find that you can save up to ninety-five percent off of products.

Another thing that you can find that can be marketed are name brand shoes. How many of you out there love name brand shoes such as Nike and Adidas? Well, you are in luck because these can be used as well. There are other things too.

Even those mini bikes that cost a fortune can be drop shipped. You would normally pay up to a thousand dollars, but when its drop shipped you don't pay nearly that amount. You only pay a hundred dollars.

Are you still looking for more? We have more than that in which you can find that you can get at a cheaper rate. The camcorder that you have been looking for that might cost over a hundred dollars. Well, now you can get it for only about eighty dollars. These are name brand as well.

So, you see, you can get some amazing deals, and if you look hard enough, you can find what you might be looking for. You can also find that most things can be drop shipped.

There are many more things than just those that can be marketed. Just you wait and see. Go on and search and we think you'd be surprised by the number of items that you learn can be drop shipped. We know that we were when we found out just how much stuff was out there for you to buy with this sort of option.

Choosing your Dropshipping Products

The greatest obstacle when it comes to dropshipping on using a Shopify store for sole businesspersons is figuring out a niche and market products to go into. But still it is no big deal that this problem is faced because it determines eventually in the long run, the success or downfall of the drop shipper and his business. There is a wrong idea that says any niche you can think of will turn out to be successful and yield good profits if embarked in, even though you have no knowledge or curiosity for whatever you would be selling.

Well, sorry to burst your bubble, but that is outrageously not true.

In a chosen niche, to be able to sense any fraud related actions and attest to the quality of the products, processes involved, fee structures or any related element, you for sure need to know your onions when it comes to that product.

How to Sell Successfully On Shopify

If your number one priority is to build a standard and productive dropshipping business online using Shopify, there are things you have to be aware of. Establishing a successful online business will require you putting away your personal passions when it comes to research and following the measures discussed below:

Get Your Hands On Privileged Charges and Distributions: If you get lucky, you can be have the advantage of getting or reaching a privileged or special agreement with the manufacture or wholesaler – whoever you choose to get your items from – to carry an item you can make profit from by selling online on your Shopify store. This can sometimes be impossible to get access to because tons of other drop shippers might also have the same access and privileges to the same good and prices.

Underprice The Items You Sell: This is one skill used mostly on Shopify and other ecommerce stores to steal customers from the accumulating lot present in the market. But this is not all that promising as it can leave you doomed to failure. If the only stunt you can pull to serve as value of the services you offer on Shopify is a low price, then you will be caught in the web of a war – since we stated clearly that it is mostly used – that would rid you of almost entirely all of your gains.

Give More Value Without Charging: Rendering priceless info that supplements the items you market is established to be one of the best ways that can be used to side line yourself positively while charging a premium price. In the world of dropshipping on Shopify, it would be no crime if you render advice expertly alongside guidance concerning products or issues relating to your niche or the items you put up for sale. At least, entrepreneurs are out there solving problems of people, so it can be done by merchants such as you on Shopify.

Images Of Products In High Definition: It would be good to make customers get the real view and feel of the product they are going ahead to purchase and this can be achieved with product images featuring a high quality. Websites such as Burst provides free to access product photos alongside some business ideas you might need to get your Shopify store in motion.

Apart from all this listed above there are still a lot when it comes to adding value to that complex niche you find hard to understand, such as:

- Offering variety among components
- Making Available a well detailed guide for buyers
- Guide creation for installation as well as setup
- Thorough video creation describing how product functions
- Providing a step by step guide system that makes components characteristics understandable

Selecting the Best Customers
The sooner you understand that all customers were created differently, the sooner you accept the strange fact that some customers wanting to make a sale of a very small product will feel entitled to ask for the moon while on the other hand, some money bags and big spending customers would almost ask for nothing.

There are clients that you would discover that are worth the time you give them and more, and these clients can only be gotten when you target the perfect demographic. This in turn can end up being the turning point for your business, providing it the catalyst it needs to take off.

The Hobbyists: These set of customers tend to spend most of their cash on the purchase of equipment, tools and machineries for themselves. Many go to Shopify, buying mountain bikes that cost more than the cars they ride just because of their love for it, a dog maniac can spend a fortune purchasing a leash or a dog accessory for their pet. If you can identify and work on the best kind of hobbyist niche and correctly connect with the lovers and their needs then without doubt, you would do very well on Shopify.

Business Clients: Most business clients turn out to be sensitive when it comes to price but that doesn't stop them from ordering in large quantities compared to individual bodies or customers. Once you have created something more than an acquaintance and earned the trust of such business clients, there is a high chance that you are walking down the road of a long-term, voluminous, positive yielding relationship. It is also possible that you can sell a product that seems appealing to both individual bodies and your business clients.

Looping Buyers: Recurring and repeated revenue is a thing of joy. On your Shopify store, if you sell a disposable material or one that needs to be reordered on a timely basis, it could help you grow faster while ensuring you build a base for your customers that return to make purchases from time to time.

Other Things to Consider At the Product Selection Phase

The Right Pricing: Be sure to put into consideration the charged fee in relation to the rate of pre-sale service that would need to be rendered by you. Many are those that would want to make purchase and would also want to have a talk with a sales representative before going ahead in making the purchase especially if it is a large one, to ensure the item in question is of good fit and to be assured of the legitimacy of the store.

What this all boils down to is that if you ever decide to put up items of high price for sale, be ready and sure that you can provide an individualized phone support. Also trying your best to make sure that the margins set in place are firm enough to reassert the pre-sale back up you will need to render.

Minimum Advertised Pricing [MAP] Billings: The minimum advertised price is something established by manufacturers for the items they supply, after which they will require of all those reselling the products should charge at a certain rate or above it. This sort of establishment by the manufacturers mitigates the price wars – which occur mostly with dropshipped items – that unexpectedly happen so as to ensure that businesspersons like you can make a substantial amount of gain by going into business with them.

If you come across a niche in which the manufacturer bears a lot of emphasis on MAP billings it would be of great advantage which is valuable if you plan on embarking on the construction of a Shopify store that would be of high value. Minding the fact that price rate would be constant and cut through all competitors, you can confidently put your weight on the strength of your Shopify website without having to be bothered about loss of profits to an inferior competition.

Sales Possibility: The best time to think of the potential and amount of returns that would be made from a business is before you kick start, not when you are knee-deep already before it reoccurs to you that getting customers to come purchase is a dying situation. Go into some deep thinking of things you can do to publicize you Shopify store, can you write articles about what you sell, organize a product giveaway, invest in email marketing, social media marketing and the likes? If all of the options listed doesn't seem to be something you can imagine yourself doing then you might need to take some more time to think in another direction.

Accompanying Accessories: Conventionally when it comes to retailing, the price margins placed on essentials are obviously higher compared to that of the high billed products. For example, a mobile phone store on Shopify hits a maximum of 5% on the margin making sales of the current brand of cellphone, but they end up hitting more than 100%, sometimes close to 200% on the margin on the accessories such as the case that goes with it.

Just like it is with every customer, they bother much about what price is delegated to the big package and care not or care less for the tag that comes along with the small accessories box. Like the illustration given above, a customer will hover round lot of shops to find the best price attached to the latest smartphone but doesn't do the same when it comes to getting the case of that phone. The customer would prefer going to the same store where the phone was bought just to purchase the case instead of going to another store just because a trusting bond has being somewhat created.

Out Of The Box Products: If you run a Shopify store where the products sold are not easily found locally, it increases you chances of prospering so far you avoid getting too precise and specific. When it gets to purchasing hammer and nails to fix the lawn they can simply walk their way to the locally existing hardware store. But when it comes to items such as a Knight's costume – the Medieval version – or equipment required for falcon training where do you think they would go?

Bigger Is Not Always Better: In the world we are in today, customers want all the luxury and keep on hoping that they get free shipment more often, this can be a very great problem if the products you put up for sale are massive in size which would turn out to be too costly for shipping. So the smaller the packages are the cheaper and easier it is to get it shipped to your clients.

With the above you will discover that picking a profitable niche is not all bed of roses and would request of you to put numerous things into consideration. The above list should educate you on the view of items up for dropshipping that would be profitable.

Step 5: Finalize Your Set Up and Launch

As a new entrepreneur in the dropshipping business, it is important that you launch your web store with impact, and prepare yourself to handle customers, set up your shipping costs, and improving your profit margin.

Use Social Media to Connect and Interact with your Target Market

Social media accounts are very important for marketing purposes and for interacting with your customers. Understand who your products are targeted at, and which is the best Social Media platform to reach out to them. As an example, if your product is targeted at teenagers, Snapchat or Pintrest might be more relevant than Facebook.

Social media has many uses beyond posting your products and selling. By creating a community around your product or brand increases the value your business provides and allows people to identify with the values and identify of the brand.

Having customers post reviews and product pictures or testimonials is also a good way to generate social proof. Seeing real people use and review your products builds confidence in other potential customers. These posts are invaluable as they get your brand and your product in view of other people without you spending a dime. Make sure your customers are happy with your product and services!

Google Analytics

This is a free solution that is incredibly full featured, and arguably better than most paid solutions in the market. When you have a webpage, it is important to track the numbers. How many visitors, when they come, and where they go on your website can give insight to what is popular, and what drives them to your business.

Having good analytics is critical to understanding your customer mindset, and that in turn leads to better serving your customer. For example, if your customers are mostly using mobile devices to access your store, you want to ensure that your web pages are optimized for mobile devices.

The data provided from running Google Analytics can also form the basis of your Search Engine Optimization (SEO) strategy. Understanding which keywords are driving people to your website allows you to plan for content and products that fall in that category. This would feedback into better data that you can use to refine the strategy as your website gains in SEO rank.

Test, Test, and Test the System Again

Even the best designed and coded websites may have bugs. Things like the layout, image sizing, and mobile device optimization should be checked several times over. You want to ensure that the result of your hard work thus far is not undermined by a single error in code.

Webforms, shopping carts, and buttons are especially prone to errors. You want to ensure these work as intended before you launch.

Broken links, or 404 pages, should be avoided as far as possible. At worst, a search bar or sitemap would hopefully help keep the customer on your website.

Customer Service Tips

If there is one key factor that will determine your success in the dropshipping business, then it has to be your reputation. It is important to give customers the best experience so that they trust you and stay loyal. Here are some best practices to remember:

- You are always responsible for everything that goes wrong. Even if the supplier messed up, you are the one the customer will blame. You need to step up and appease the customer, even if it means losing money. You do not want to risk getting negative reviews.

- Understand what customers want and need. Ensure a secure checkout system and keep their personal information protected. Make your website professional and user-friendly. If possible, provide customers with a way to track their order without having to contact you all the time.

- Be knowledgeable about your products. Create detailed product descriptions, FAQ pages, and even a newsletter to give customers access to more information. This will help you come across as an expert.

- Always keep your customers happy. Happy customers are repeat customers who go out and spread the word to others. Treat your customers well.

- Avoid having back orders. Imagine if a customer makes an order for a product and after contacting the supplier, they inform you that the product is out of stock. You are now left with the task of explaining to the customer why you cannot fulfill their order. This is a back order, and it can lead to negative feedback and lost sales. To avoid this kind of scenario, you can decide to stock some items at home. In case of a back order, you sell your stock and then ask the supplier to send you the item when they have restocked. Alternatively, you should have a backup supplier in case the first supplier does not come through in time.

Tips for Optimizing Shipping Costs

When you launch your dropshipping business, you have to establish a proper shipping strategy. Your shipping charges will affect whether a customer completes a transaction or not. The problem you have is that you have no control over the actual shipping cost – the supplier does.

So what do you do?

You can find out what your competitors are charging and then you set up a standard shipping policy. Here are some strategies:

- Offer customers free shipping – Customers expect this nowadays. However, you can advertise "free" shipping and then add your shipping cost to the MSRP so that the customer pays for it anyway.

- Offer a flat rate – Group your products according to a particular weight and price range and then offer that entire range of products a flat rate for shipping. Once your sales improve, you can look at fast-moving product ranges and increase your shipping charges.

Your online dropshipping store is now ready! All you have to do now is do away with the password protection that you had set up on your website. Go ahead and send out tweets, Facebook posts, and emails to your contacts to generate traffic to your store.

Step 6: Advertising and Promotion

Choose Profitable Source of Traffic

Traffic is the most important thing when it comes to generating your income and profit. There are many ways to bring traffic to your website. But unfortunately, not every way brings the same type of visitors.

The purpose of this is that you should actively test and compare your sources of traffic and concentrate on those that are bringing your the best results.

First of all, you should use your brain here and advertise yourself on those sites that have content relevant to yours. For example, if you are getting lots of traffic from social bookmarking sites - the chances are you won't see a lot of profit. You will be lucky if you see a few bucks.

But at the same time, if you are advertising through Google AdWords or if you are doing good search engine optimization, chances are that your return on investment will be good. That will happen because your visitors will be looking for content on your website.

So what to do next?

It's simple, compare those sources of traffic income and decide which ones are worth your time. My advice is that you should focus on 3 sources the most. That will give you the opportunity to get the most out of it.

And also, don't forget that you should never stop testing different sources of income because results might surprise you. Test everything on a small scale and then see if it's worth going for it if you increase your efforts.

After you found profitable income of visitors and costumers, you could try to test again those sites that didn't pass your norm at the beginning, especially if you made tweaks to your sales page.

Build Website Authority and Credibility with SEO

After building the Shopify store and you put everything in place ready for your dropshipping business, you might have problems getting the right kind of people or the right amount of people to view your store. This is where getting a website authority is important as well as getting website credibility.

We mentioned Search Engine Optimization in preceding chapters, well this where they are really put into place and what makes them more than valuable to ecommerce businesspersons in the online world where ads charges keeps on getting expensive every day. Unfortunately but as expected, there are thousands – probably tens of thousands – of other stores on Shopify that offer and sell the same products as you do so the important question is how do search engines know which store to show first when your niche is looked up?

This is a job for the off-page SEO and other elements that make it up, which goes telling the search engine what store is more relevant and of more value. A more crucial of these results come from backlinks. Backlinks refer to links that redirects or points to your store from other websites. So in this chapter we are going to be discussing how backlinks can help your website/Shopify store gain authority and enough credibility.

The Types of Backlinks

The first thing to note about backlinks is that **not all backlinks are created equal.** The two types of backlinks are the *follow backlinks* and the *nofollow backlinks.*

The follow backlinks are the kind of simple links from a website to your website/Shopify store that in a way tells the search engine "I can vouch for this website". On the other hand, the nofollow backlink is a link in which the person giving the redirecting link uses a code telling the bots: "This website exists, that's all I know. I am not endorsing them though".

To make a backlink a follow or nofollow backlink, it relies on the author of the HTML of the website to add an extra bit of text to make it whatever kind of backlink you prefer it to be.

Another thing to note when it comes to backlinks is that some backlinks worth more than other backlinks. As we established earlier that no backlinks are created equal, when we talk about worth of backlinks it simply means each backlinks are like upvotes for your site/store but a link from BBC is worth more than a link from some personal blog that was started barely months ago. But not minding all these, there are also other factors that determine the worth of a link:

When your link is used on sites with unique domains, it serves as more important ti sites that have in previous times being linked to you.

Links are also of more value and relevance when it is embedded beneath keyword rich texts. For example, a link embedded beneath texts like "advanced men's motor bikes" are of more value than links embedded beneath the common "click here" texts.

Also a web page containing numerous numbers of links on it will end up passing less value per links included.

All this establishes the authority that a website has compared against others, especially now that you have learnt how much worth a link from a website means to you.

There are a number of ways known to make backlinks work more effectively or well applied. Many have also proven to work but the most effective of all of them are:

Getting Your Posts Reviewed: This is one of the known ways to getting increased traffic on your Shopify store and getting backlinks. This can be made possible by reaching out to real bloggers to have your Shopify store's product reviewed on their page as this is a known way to garner a link back to your site almost naturally.

Beforehand, you would have to get yourself familiar with various blogs and discovering their niche and how large they are [For worth-wise consideration]. Take your time to build a relationship with the authors by engaging with all their updated posts to get yourself noticed. When an acquaintance has been achieved then let them in on your products and express how happy you would be if they could let their audience know about it.

Get Your Manufacturer To Give You A Link: Many ecommerce merchants that engage in selling on Shopify stores have realized that it makes more sense if you are provided with a backlink from the website of the manufacturers whose product you are going to be selling. All it takes is a polite mail requesting them to have you included in directory of partners or resellers.

Link building is essential in getting an authoritative and credible website. Search engines basically need others to endorse you and that is what backlinks are responsible for. Dedicate just a few hours every week to building links and as times goes by, you would have built a sturdy Shopify store delivering a steady traffic streaming in, each and every day.

Email Marketing

Once you have traffic on your website you can get visitors to sign up for your newsletter for an incentive, such as a coupon codes or freebies on their next order, in exchange for their email address.

Email marketing is amazing because it's so high converting, plus it's also the most personal sort of marketing. With email marketing, the trick is to provide value and not just constantly sell. If you're going to do email marketing, you have to provide value in some sale, such as a fire sale to get rid of stock.

Social Media

Let's face it; social media is one of the greatest marketing tools of our time. If for some reason, you are unaware of or just not using social media to get the word out about your store, you could be missing out on thousands of sales. The average American checks his or her social media pages constantly throughout the day. That's ongoing potential exposure for your site.

The whole idea behind marketing your product on social media is not to get folks to rush out and buy your product now. The main purpose is product awareness. Let the emotional buying process start when they land on your Shopify page.

Every share reaches a great number of people. That equals more product awareness.

The process is straightforward. The majority of themes already have social media buttons built in, and while editing your site, you can link them to your business' social accounts. You can also search and find the button codes and instructions if you wanted to edit the code manually. Tech support should be able to guide you as well. Each social site will have a code and may also give instructions.

One of the best ways to generate sales via social media is to have your customers do your marketing for you, for free. By adding the AddThis App, you customers can now become your marketing team. By sharing your site with their friends, you can reach thousands of extra potential customers. The app is linked to all the most popular social network sites and uses over seventy languages.

Facebook Ads

You should also run some Facebook ads so you can get the word out about your store. There are two main types. One is website conversion, and the other is pay per click.

Conclusion

In this book, we've looked at what drop shipping is, how it works and who is involved in the supply chain. We've also looked at how you need to select your niche and product and how to determine which suppliers are the best. I've given you the information you need to start your own business and what sales channels are available to you.

I hope that this book was helpful for you. Retail sales using drop shipping is a fairly common theme these days, so you need every edge you can get before you venture into this market. I hope that this book has provided you with at least some of those edges.

If you have been considering whether this is the right business to help you earn some passive income, now you know.

The next step is to start doing the work necessary to set up your business. It will not do you any good to read this book and not take action. Start researching which niche market to go into and move on from there. It is very fulfilling knowing that you are making money from home and earning a decent income online.

www.ingramcontent.com/pod-product-compliance
Lightning Source LLC
Chambersburg PA
CBHW070410230526
45471CB00006B/2729